Bless the Beasts:
Pet Parables
For Kids Of All Ages

Marilyn Holasek Lloyd

ISBN: 1512319090
ISBN 13: 9781512319095
Library of Congress Control Number: 2015908230
CreateSpace Independent Publishing Platform
North Charleston, South Carolina

DEDICATION:

This book is dedicated to Peyton Thomas Lloyd, Carter Patrick Lloyd, Meredith Addington Lloyd, Jacob William Saunders, Grayson Lloyd Saunders, and to their pet-loving Opa, Thomas Stacy Lloyd Jr., MD.

Beasts as pets have been loved by generations of children as well as adults. They teach us about themselves and ourselves. Therefore, I also dedicate these parables to all of those beasts who have enriched the lives of my family and families everywhere.

A parable is a story that is used to teach a moral lesson. These parables are stories about my pets as well as the pets of my family and friends.

What makes these pet parables unique is that they are all true stories, but I did take some artistic license with the stories written in the first person.

Parables are usually about people, but in almost every case, my parables involve the owner of the pet just as much as the pets themselves. Pets and their owners share a loving and caring relationship. But this involves both benefits and joy along with sacrifice and responsibility.

ACKNOWLEDGMENTS

In 1989, Dr. Sue Hanna and Dr. Glen Thomas (Mary Washington College) were my mentors on the original graduate project, the writing of *Bless the Beasts: Pet Parables for Kids of All Ages.* I am eternally grateful to them.

My husband, Dr. Thomas Stacy Lloyd, Jr., delighted in and helped to nurture all of the many pets we adopted through the decades. He generously provided for all the beasts and some of their veterinary care was very expensive. He always encouraged me in all of my education and endeavors. He was my first editor, my best friend, and my beloved husband for almost 35 years.

My children, William Stacy Lloyd and Holly Marilyn Lloyd Saunders, learned as many lessons from these beasts as I did. They truly supported me through good times and bad and in sickness and in health. My children and husband were crucial to my recovery from breast cancer in1996.

My brother, Jonathan Holasek, has been my constant medical advocate since 1996, and always provides insight, encouragement, and support.

Sally Gould was invaluable in helping me update and edit all the parables including the 5 new ones. She was my daily cheerleader and friend. And I am eternally grateful.

Marian Hailey-Moss, the author of many books, inspired and guided me.

Create Space provided invaluable help with the publishing process and graphic arts for this book.

My son-in-law, Jeff Saunders, helped with images.

My friend, Anita Holle, painted the picture of Gobble.

Marilyn Perry, my friend, helped care for many of these pets.

My cousin, Carol Wilson, helped with the final revisions.

The Holasek family taught me my morals and values. Without them, I would not be the person I am today, since my beloved mother, Mildred, died when I was an infant. The picture of the rabbit on the cover is of the actual paper mache rabbit that was in the Holasek family grocery/butcher shop window in Cleveland in the early 1900s. This rabbit honors the original Holasek family: Grandpa Josef, Grandma Theresa, my father William, Aunt Theresa, Aunt Josephine, Uncle Joe, Uncle Fred, Aunt Lillian, Uncle George, and Uncle Ed.

I LOVE YOU, TOO, BRUTUS

Be gentle and ready to forgive; never hold grudges.
—Colossians 4:13

The realization came to me that I was a dog when my mistress gave birth to the animals. Until that time, I, Brutus Lloyd, had a place by the table, on the bed, and in the hearts of my master and mistress.

After the animals came—first a male, then a female—my place became under the table, under the bed, and under the hearts of my master and mistress. I missed the tidbits, but most of all, I missed the attention and love. I was depressed for a long time.

To cope all those years with a difficult situation, I resorted to destructive behavior. I was house trained, but I intentionally went into the dining room to wet on the rug. This behavior continued until I realized the animals were here to stay.

I decided to give the animals a chance. I would nuzzle up close to them, but as infants, they tried to pull the hair out of my back. They were lucky I didn't try to bite them. At that point, I made the decision not to go near either of the animals again.

It was then I realized that I needed a different tactic. I knew how many times my mistress took the animals to the doctors. Maybe I could get my mistress's attention by getting sick. I found a gang of fleas in the backyard, and I would rub my back into them. This always caused a flea allergy that irritated my skin to the point of bleeding. Then I would get the mistress's attention and be taken to the vet.

I refused to eat my dog bones and ended up with an abscessed tooth. That didn't work out as I planned, because I ended up with one less tooth, and that caused me a lot of pain. My trips to the vet were not worth the extra attention.

If this wasn't bad enough, true disaster really struck. One day the animals found a kitten in the backyard. I wasn't too worried, because I always heard my mistress say, "I hate cats. There will never be a cat in my house." The animals started wailing and crying, and the mistress let the kitten stay. If only the kitten hadn't been so cute. Why did he have to have four white paws? Why couldn't he have been full of disease or something? The kitten soon became a cat, and I got even less attention than before. The two animals gave the cat a lot of attention. I was really jealous. I became more and more depressed.

Every chance I had, I would crawl under the fence and sit in the road, hoping for a new family. I always got picked up by some loving people and returned home, or I was taken to the dog pound. Sometimes I wished that my mistress would just take off my nametag, and I could get a chance with a new family.

No such luck, so I tried a different tactic. I increased my acting-out behavior. I ate all the garbage I could get my paws on. I started wetting in other places in the house to map out my territory from the cat. I escaped to chase girl dogs in heat. That was a mistake. I was taken to the vet to have a little operation. Little? Heck no! I came home barking in a higher voice, and I lost my interest for girl dogs.

I felt I had really sunk to an all-time low. Nothing was working in my life. This was when I decided I had to forgive the animals for being born, and move on with my life.

Amazing things happened after I forgave the animals. They started paying more attention to me. I got tidbits from the table. I got to sleep in their beds, and they stroked and petted and loved me.

I even learned how to deal with my feelings of jealousy for the cat and the three kittens that followed. I realized how

foolish I had been to nurture my feelings of jealousy and hostility. I knew how far I had come when just the other day, I found myself napping next to Whitepaws and one of the kittens.

Just about that time, the girl animal named Holly came up to all of us, stroked the cats, and then turned to me and gave me a kiss, saying, "I love you, too, Brutus."

MORAL

Live to forgive! Because up and on is better than down and under.

ADOPTING PRETTY LADY

God has given us different gifts for doing certain things well.
—Romans 12:6

I went with my wife to buy her a collie for a wedding present, priding myself on being a good judge of champion dogs. When we arrived at the collie farm, the breeder showed us a beautiful tricolor collie.

When the collie first glanced at me, she really liked me. She ran up to me, nuzzled my arm, and stared at me in an endearing way with sparkly eyes. Both my wife and I were taken in by this collie's attraction to me. The sale was made, and we took the collie to our home.

On arriving home, the collie continued to give me all of this adoring attention until I took off my new Turkish leather jacket. Swiftly, the collie ran up to the jacket and nuzzled it and loved it.

I realized it was Lady's profound sense of smell that attracted her to that leather jacket. It is a powerful gift that all dogs have. This gift allows them to distinguish friend or foe, be a rescue dog, and even sniff out cancer.

Lady used her gift to find herself a home.

Some years later, Lady Lloyd of the Woods was entered in a beautiful dog contest at the dog mart. The judge wore a leather jacket. Lady *won*!

MORAL

Dogs can win a life and a contest by a nose!

THE CARE OF PRETTY LADY

*I expect to pass through this world but once. Any good therefore that
I can do, or any kindness or abilities that I can show to any fellow
creature, let me do it now. Let me not defer it or neglect it, for I shall
not pass this way again.*
—William Penn

Lady Lloyd of the Woods, nick-
named Pretty Lady, was a beautiful dog by anyone's standards.
A long-haired tricolored collie,
Pretty Lady had a very thick
coat of hair with an undercoat.

Lady's family, who desired a collie from reading books about
Lassie and Shep the dog, never
considered the care and main-
tenance of a collie.

Collies' thick coats of hair need constant attention. Daily
brushing and trips to the dog groomer are necessary to maintain their coat.

When the children came into this family, the priorities of the family changed dramatically. What little time they devoted to grooming and caring for Pretty Lady became less and less. The dog deserved more time, not less. After all, she was a very good watchdog, loved those children, and guarded them in the yard.

Because of this lack of attention, Pretty Lady's hair got so matted at times that she needed to be shaved down to bare skin in the summer. Pretty Lady looked like a goat!

Pretty Lady would hide in embarrassment. She was so humiliated by this "hairless" state of affairs over which she had no control.

The family learned a major lesson at the expense of this beautiful dog. They learned that it was not fair to the dog to not appropriate the time and effort needed to keep Pretty Lady beautiful and healthy.

The family vowed never to make that mistake again with another dog.

And they didn't.

MORAL

Heed the needs of the breed.

WHITEPAWS, THE CAT WHO LEARNED HOW TO LOVE

Love lifted me; love lifted me. When nothing else could help, love lifted me.
—From a hymn by Howard E. Smith

A young kitten watched as one by one his brothers and sisters were thrown from a moving car onto the cold and hard asphalt of a battlefield park drive. Soon it was his turn. The mean driver flung him from the car, saying, "Good riddance."

The kitten shivered as he suffered from the cold and an empty feeling in his stomach. "Is this all there is to life?" he wondered. He tried to keep moving to keep warm and to not think about food. He wandered into a fenced-in yard where a big dog frightened him up a tree.

Out of the nearby house came a woman, who picked up this kitten and took him into the house. Even though the woman fed him milk and other nutritious food, he didn't trust her. For one thing, he sensed she didn't like cats.

After he ate as much as he could, he ran into the corner to hide. He stayed there until a small boy and girl came running into the room and picked him up and gently stroked him. The children asked the woman if he could stay. She said, "Absolutely not." And she added, "We have two dogs." So, she began calling the SPCA to find him another home. The kitten could tell by the tone of her voice that he was right. She didn't like cats.

The SPCA told the woman to take a number to have the kitten put to sleep. The little boy and girl started crying and carrying on. Then the father came home from work. The kitten could tell he liked cats. Being outnumbered and having pity on the kitten, the woman relented and said he could stay.

The children were so happy. The woman always said it was the four white paws on the cute kitten and their father's intervention that had saved him. The kitten was called Whitepaws, and a new chapter in his life began.

The family needed to be very patient with Whitepaws because he was aloof, mistrustful, and not yet capable of showing love. They gave him a lot of attention, stroking, petting, and talking to him.

The family's collie ignored the cat, and the little dog seemed jealous.

But ever so gradually, Whitepaws warmed up to the family. At first, Whitepaws would come near everybody only at mealtime, against their legs.

After a few weeks, he would come and sit with the children in their rooms while they did their homework. Soon he was spending time with each child before he or she fell asleep. He began to purr.

When the little girl had the flu, the kitten stayed next to her until she got better. He even sat with the woman when she was ill. And he provided comfort to the little boy when he was upset and crying.

Whitepaws knew what suffering was all about. But most of all, he learned what love was all about. He wanted to pass it on.

MORAL

Love lifted even a cat.

DUDE, THE ROCK FETCHING DOG

There is a time for everything, and a season for every activity under heaven. . . A time to scatter stones, and a time to gather them...
—Ecclesiastes 3:1, 5

Dude, a shepherd retriever, was a dog who liked to carry things. However, his original owners taught him to fetch rocks instead of sticks and balls. He became skillful, even obsessed, in rock collecting. Luckily, his new owners lived on top of a creek bed, so Dude never had to look far for any size rock that he wanted.

For Dude, each rock size had a different meaning. The small ones, he chewed on like bones. The medium-size rocks he placed at the doorway so that anyone coming out of the door couldn't miss them and would be sure to throw them.

He saved the large rocks for those times when someone was outside but wouldn't throw a rock for him to fetch. He would retrieve the biggest rock he could find and drop it on the unsuspecting victim's foot. When that happened, the victim would usually throw the rock, shouting loudly. Dude didn't understand the words, but he enjoyed the sound of the voice and showing off his skill.

Dude especially liked it when the owner had to have work done outside of the house, such as house painting or window washing. He would pile his rocks at the bottom of the worker's ladder, waiting for the action when the worker came down from the ladder.

Each new day meant a new rock search for Dude. He fetched rocks from morning to night, clutching each one as though his life depended upon it. Anyone who knew Dude never saw him without a rock held snugly between his teeth unless he was resting or eating.

As the years went by, Dude took his rock talent to the extreme. He seemed like a "rockaholic," never resting, always obsessed by the task at hand, which was to find the next rock. He felt he had a problem, but he just couldn't stop. He watched the other dogs in his family enjoying life, but Dude never took the time to enjoy a romp in the woods or to bask in the sun. He never went on quiet walks or even chased a butterfly like the other dogs. Rocks were all that mattered to Dude.

Where did this all lead?

Dude, in his old age, had to eat watered-down canned dog food because he wore down his teeth from chewing on all those rocks. He was unable to enjoy a steak or even a dog bone. Dude had to be content with gumming his food for the rest of his life.

MORAL

Don't let your talents grind you down.

REBEL

If you can gain your freedom, do so.
—1 Corinthians 1:21

Not all dogs conform to the pattern of a loyal family pet. Some of us are born with a spirit that longs to be free. I am such a beast. Although I love my young master, Philip, very much, I yearn for the wide-open spaces. This is a problem since I live in a city with a leash law. Many times Philip has had to bail me out of the local dog pound for roaming the city streets.

This changed when Philip and I moved to a new house with a chain-link fence. Philip thought that now my roaming days were over. However, I soon learned to escape either by jumping over, digging under, or just waiting until someone accidentally left the gate open.

It was then that Philip tried closing me in the basement during part of the day. However, I would scratch and howl at the door until he would let me out. Out of desperation, he chained me outside. That time, I broke the chain loose and followed him into town, chain and all.

Finally, when Philip realized it was impossible for me to be a house pet, he allowed me to go free. He felt comfortable with his decision because by then I had become "street smart" and wise to the dogcatcher. I knew the sounds, looks, and smells of the dogcatcher's truck. He could have dangled a juicy steak and I wouldn't be lured into his truck.

Also, Philip learned of my daily rounds from the garbage man. A garbage truck came for an additional pickup. Philip was home from school, and the garbage man exclaimed, "Oh, this is where that little white dog lives. We always wondered because we see him every day."

Philip also learned that my first stop after prancing down the park road would be to meet the city workers at the city shop for a tidbit in the morning. Then, in nice weather, I might sun myself by the canal before visiting friends by the railroad track. Later in the afternoon, I would revisit the city shop for an afternoon snack. Finally, in a last burst of energy before dinner, I might chase a few cats before coming home.

One day, one of the cats I chased daily started chasing me. I learned I couldn't climb a telephone pole like a cat!

After such a tiring day, I am ready for a quiet night with Philip. Everyone gets what he wants. I am free by day, and Philip gets a home-loving dog, at least for the night.

MORAL

Every dog that has his days might give you his nights.

GIDGET, THE PIGGISH DACHSHUND

Bad habits are like chains that are too light to feel until they are too heavy to carry.
—Warren Buffet

A family adopted an overweight, piggish dachshund named Gidget.

It was not Gidget's fault that she had a habit of eating too much. It was the previous owner who allowed Gidget to have this unhealthy habit.

Anyone who has ever owned a dachshund knows that they were bred for their long backs to be badger hunters. However, it is of utmost importance for dachshunds to maintain a weight that their back can carry.

Although her new owners tried to restrict her food intake, Gidget used any excuse she could to keep her habit going of eating more and more. If it were particularly cold outside, this would give Gidget an excuse to raid the garbage can in the kitchen. If it were hot outside, she would raid the garbage can in the backyard and then come into the air-conditioning to rest. If the weather were perfect, she would take a walk to raid the neighbor's garbage cans while reasoning to herself that she was getting exercise before and after eating.

When there was no garbage to find anywhere, Gidget found other amazing ways to get something to eat and reinforce her habit. Her owners loved to eat pistachios. Although they were quite a challenge, she soon learned how to crack the nuts and leave the shells.

Gidget particularly looked forward to houseguests, because that meant extra people from whom to beg for food.

At one Halloween party, Gidget learned to eat apples. After bobbing for apples, the guests would usually place their apples next to them. Gidget would grab each apple and run to the door. After eating the fruit, she would return and snatch up another until she had eaten about six apples before the guests became wise to her tactics.

While the partygoers laughed so hard at this fat dog running out of the room looking like a suckling pig, Gidget got to eat four more apples. She didn't care if they laughed; the food was all that mattered.

Finding food for her habit on quiet days at home became especially difficult. It was at these times that Gidget resorted to eating things that looked like food. She started eating gum. She learned how to open plastic antacid containers and eat the pills.

Gidget's owners realized that something drastic needed to be done to break her piggish habit because it was causing her many physical problems. All of this was no laughing matter. Gidget actually needed several operations to deal with the results of her over-eating. After her care from the veterinarian, Gidget was fed a healthy diet, and all other sources of food and things that looked like food were removed from her immediate environment.

Gidget never looked better and felt better! Her owners helped her to overcome her bad habit and showed her that change was possible. She just needed a lot of support and help.

MORAL

The journey to good habits can be long, but what matters is the help you get along the way.

A BOY AND HIS DUCKS: DOPEY AND DOC

For each will have to bear his own load.
—Galatians 6:5

When Tom was ten years old, he wanted a pair of pet ducklings because all of his friends were getting them at Easter. Tom said he would take very good care of them. He would feed them and do anything it took to have those ducks. His mother tried to talk him out of getting ducks, because it might not work out well for the ducks. It was well known that getting pets at holiday time was a bad idea. However, Tom insisted, and with motherly resignation, his mother bought him two cute ducklings, which he named Dopey and Doc.

Dopey and Doc fit nicely in the enamel tub in the backyard and enjoyed swimming around, quacking quietly to themselves. The ducklings caused the family little trouble even though the yard was fenced only on three sides. They never wandered off to investigate their surroundings even though they lived in a big city.

Unfortunately, Dopey and Doc grew up to be big white ducks. The bigger they grew, the louder they got, until the mother started calling them Squeaky and Squawky. The noise of their quacking became very annoying, but their loud voices were not the only problem. They outgrew the enamel tub and their duck house, and with cold weather coming, the mother was worried about what to do with the ducks.

All of these problems came to a head around the Christmas holidays. Between school and holiday anticipation, Tom was too busy to properly care for Dopey and Doc. His mother had to do all the feeding and cleaning up after them. She was getting very impatient.

This impatient mother told the boy if those ducks caused her any more problems, they would have to go. Later that same week, the missing duck episode began.

Another boy in the neighborhood, who was also ignoring his ducks, let his ducks get loose in the neighborhood. This boy's mother went looking for their ducks and saw Dopey and Doc and took them to her house.

Meanwhile, Tom's mother noticed that Dopey and Doc were missing and went looking for them. She found the other boy's ducks, who raised a big ruckus and almost bit her.

After a long search, Dopey and Doc saw Tom's mother from several yards away. They called to her with their quacking and squawking to come and rescue them. A motherly duck exchange was made. Dopey and Doc smiled at the mother as they waddled home.

However, they weren't smiling for long, because when the boy came home from school, the mother reminded him of her warning. She told him it was a mistake getting those ducks on a holiday whim and the ducks had to go. Despite the boy's tears and protests, Dopey and Doc were sent away, never to return.

MORAL

Pet care is a job; do it or you will sob.

THE HOUSE CATS THAT PRACTICED CATCHING MICE

Practice makes perfect.
—An old proverb by unknown author

———————

Day and night, four playful cats romped around their family's home. These cats were considered to be "house cats" because they were never allowed to go outside. The owner decided to confine them to the house for their own protection.

Luckily, the house was big enough that the cats had plenty of places to hide, look out the windows, and chase one another. The cats not only got along very well, but they also achieved a sense of peace with the several dogs that also lived in the house.

Whitepaws, Smokey, Tigger, and Prissy were the most happy cats, receiving much attention and love from the children and the adults who lived in the house. Life was good, except for one thing. What was missing was the cats' adventure in catching their own food—mice!

Nevertheless, all four cats seemed to remember the skill of finding and pouncing on mice, as they practiced this skill several times a day. They stalked one another as well as small items in the house. They all seemed to be full of purpose, secrets, and enjoyment as they practiced for the day that they would catch some mice.

It was the boy cat, Whitepaws, who took the practice of catching mice to a new level. In Whitepaws's mind, he equated mice with pens. Fortunately for Whitepaws, there were pens in every room of the big house. So, Whitepaws, in the middle of the night, when the family and other cats and dogs were sleeping, would roam around the rooms of the house and remove the pens from the storage containers and play with them on the floor. He would pretend that they were mice and chase them all around. He did this night after night. This was Whitepaws's opportunity to have fun and practice at the same time.

Once in a while, the family would catch Whitepaws practicing with pens and walking around with a pen in his mouth. He especially liked the pile of pens in the upstairs hallway. In the morning, these pens would be all lined up like a "kill" of a mouse family.

Well, one day a mouse family that wasn't paying attention to where they were going to live moved their residence to this family's home. Before the owner of the house could even get to the store to buy mousetraps, Whitepaws finally had his chance!

In the morning, when the family woke up, there was Whitepaws proudly standing over his present to the family. Whitepaws had pounced on and killed six mice and lined them up in a row, just like he had practiced with the pens.

MORAL

If practice is fun, the battle is won.

MAMA GERBIL

A true friend is always loyal.
—Proverbs 17:17

 I am a Mongolian desert rat, otherwise known as a gerbil. I think they named us gerbils because people would be reluctant to buy a rat at a pet store.

Gerbils arrived in the pet stores around forty-five years ago. It was about the same time when my owner-to-be went to a pet store looking for a pet. She lived in an apartment and couldn't keep a dog. So she wanted a hamster, a white mouse, or maybe a rabbit—that is, until she saw me.

I admit I am a cute gerbil. I have a brownish-gray coat and blue-green eyes with an alert and intelligent air that is very appealing.

I immediately had a new owner. She took me to her apartment, and we became friends. She spent a lot of time with me teaching me tricks with my special wheels. She always kept my cage spotlessly clean, which isn't hard because gerbils are clean animals and we don't smell bad like hamsters or mice.

Occasionally, my owner would let me run loose, and I would run up and down her arm in a playful way.

After a few months, my owner provided me with Papa Gerbil, and we began having many families. She would separate the baby gerbils from us, placing the babies in their own cage, because, admittedly, I do have a tendency to eat them. In time, my owner became an expert at raising gerbils and would sell the babies back to the pet shop.

Around the same time, my owner struck up a friendship with a woman who lived in a nearby apartment. They started spending a lot of time together doing laundry, taking walks, and sitting by the swimming pool. It was a good beginning of a friendship.

My owner did not tell her new friend about having pet gerbils. And this new friend did not know that people kept Mongolian desert rats as pets. (We were always kept hidden from view in the back bedroom.)

One day when my owner was cleaning our cages, her new friend paid an unexpected visit. When my owner went to let her friend into apartment, she accidentally left not only the baby gerbil cage open, but also the door to the bedroom.

While both women talked in the living room, my owner's friend began to squirm in her seat. Her hands started shaking, and she kept glancing over her shoulder. Finally, she couldn't contain herself any longer, and she said to my owner, "I hate to tell you this, but you have rats!"

My owner calmly replied, "Oh, they're not rats; they are my pets," as she jumped up and began catching the baby gerbils by their tails. This is the correct way to handle baby gerbils.

But then one of the baby gerbils suddenly swung up and bit my owner on her finger and blood started to run down it.

Horrified, her friend shrieked, "Oh my goodness, you were bitten by a rat! How could you keep a rat for a pet? Are you crazy?"

My owner tried to explain about having gerbils as pets, but her friend was too busy running out the door to listen. This now ex-friend never visited or spoke to my owner again.

MORAL

It is better to have a rat for a friend than a friend who is a rat.

CASEY, THE HOPEFUL HAMSTER

What is faith? It is the confident assurance that something we want is going to happen. It is the certainty that what we hope for is waiting for us, even though we cannot see it up ahead.
—Hebrews 10:1

———————

 Casey was a nosy little hamster whose curious nature always got him into trouble. He wasn't content to spend his days sitting in his cage or spinning on his wheel. He wanted to experience life outside the cage. Sometimes the children would take Casey out to play, which were his favorite times.

One time, when Casey was taken out of his cage to play, one of the children forgot about him and he found himself stuck in the couch. In order to get out of the couch, he clawed and scratched until he chewed a hole right through the couch. Luckily, Casey lived with a loving family who forgave him and had the couch repaired.

Casey's curiosity continued to cause this family a lot of grief when he would escape from his cage. He would get himself in the worst predicaments. One time, he crawled through the heater duct and found himself stuck between the walls of the family's house. Casey waited patiently for the family to help him out. Fortunately, the family was clever, and they stuffed socks through the heat register so that Casey could climb on the socks to get out.

Having faith that the family would keep trying to rescue him, Casey managed to escape again, and he climbed back between the walls of the home. However, this time he became totally stuck. The family was very upset, because they could not figure out a way to rescue Casey short of knocking holes in their rented house.

All day the mother worked to free Casey. She first tried the sock maneuver, but that didn't work. Then she drilled a tiny hole and sent a fishing line down to Casey with a piece of cheese. That didn't work either. Next, she tied the fishing line to an empty toilet paper tube to make a space capsule for Casey to climb into. That failed as well. He seemed to be hopelessly lodged in the wall.

Finally, in desperation she started drilling other holes in the wall, but she couldn't find the right place to drill. Even though Casey kept scratching and squeaking to guide her, it was hard to find his exact position.

Eight hours and many holes later, the mother drilled a hole close enough to Casey's position to save him. First his little pink hamster nose appeared and then his whiskers. Happily, he climbed out of the hole with a smile on his face, and he seemed to say, "I knew you would come!"

MORAL

When you are stuck in a wall, the only way to look is up!

PETE, AUNT LIL'S EXTRAORDINARY PARAKEET

Do not wait until some deed of greatness you may do;
Do not wait to shed your light afar;
To the many duties ever near you now be true,
Brighten the corner where you are.
—From a hymn by Charles H. Gabriel

Aunt Lil found a sad-looking, homeless parakeet in her backyard and named him Pete. Pete was an ordinary parakeet. All day long he would sit in his cage fluffing his greenish-yellow feathers. Once in a while, he would chirp or tweet, but other than that, he just sat there.

Now, Aunt Lil was not a professional bird trainer, but she was an animal lover, and she always wanted to teach a parakeet to talk. So she began working with Pete every day. She began repeating words to him like *hello, mom, doggie, Ricky,* and *birdie.* Soon, Pete learned to repeat the words, but Aunt Lil wasn't content to stop there. She went on to teach him phrases like "good morning," "good night," "hello, girls," and "Ricky, on the paper!"

Pete soon learned the phrases, and instead of Aunt Lil easing up on her training of Pete, she spent even more time teaching Pete to say full sentences. He would say, "Hello, girls. What's new?" and "Ricky, go sit on the carpet!"

Sometimes Aunt Lil would teach Pete tricks while he was talking in sentences. When she put buttons on the table, Pete would knock them one by one on the floor and say, "Bombs away."

When she let Pete fly around the living room, she would say, "Pete, time to go to sleep." He would repeat, "Time to go to sleep," and then fly back into his cage saying, "Cover me up, cover me up. It's time for bed."

When Christmastime came, Aunt Lil surprised her family by getting Pete to say a few words in Bohemian like *"Jak se máš?"* or "How are you?" He even learned to say, "Happy holidays, Holasek family." All of the relatives were astounded at this extraordinary parakeet.

MORAL

The difference between ordinary and extraordinary is that big extra!

RICKY, THE BEAGLE WHO NEVER GREW UP

Hear, O Lord, when I cry with my voice; have mercy also upon me, and answer me.
—Psalms 27:11

Ricky was a beagle who, from the time of puppyhood, became very upset when he was left alone. He would tear up anything in sight, but most of all, he would sit in his chair and sob and slobber until his owners came home. They thought he would outgrow this insecure behavior, but he didn't.

After his puppy stage, he continued to agonize and cry whenever he was alone in the house. In fact, as time passed, his crying was so bad that his entire chair in the basement would be soaked with tears.

To help Ricky cope, his owners would take him everywhere that they could. He didn't mind sitting in the car in cool weather while they were shopping or visiting. He didn't mind being outside of the house while his owners were inside. Ricky just didn't like being left all alone in the house.

However, Ricky's loneliness and separation anxiety became a real problem when the owners had to be away for extended periods of time, such as when they went to church or worked at the voting polls. His owners worried so much about Ricky that they began driving him to relatives for dog sitting.

The owners received a lot of criticism for this practice. People would say, "Why do you do it?" or "He's only a dog, you know." Despite these criticisms, they relentlessly kept Ricky happy by keeping him dependent. Even when they moved to the suburbs, they added twenty minutes going and coming from their destination to provide companionship for Ricky. His owners continued this escorting service for fourteen years until the day he died.

Were they wrong to cater to Ricky in this way? If Ricky was happy, and they were happy with this arrangement, does it matter?

MORAL

If you cry to the right people, you won't drown in your tears.

THE POSSUM WHO THOUGHT SHE WAS A PET

She gives no thought to the way of life; her paths wander aimlessly, but she does not know it.
—Proverbs 5:6

———————

Nature wisely created leafy woods as a habitat (a place to live) for wild animals, like possums.

But one possum, Mama Possum, wasn't content to just live in the backyard of a home near the woods. She viewed the pet dogs going in and out of the house, and she could hear the meows of the pet cats coming from the house. Why not a pet possum living in a house?

Scouting around the house, she spied a hole from the garage to the basement of the house. She crept through the hole to the basement and found a special safe spot there to have her babies.

Unknown to the family living in the house, Mama Possum must have been going in and out of the basement during the day to get food for herself. Being a marsupial, she must have carried the babies in her pouch for a month and then on her back for several more months.

One night, the woman of the house heard some high-pitched squeaks coming from the basement. Rushing down the steps, she discovered tiny little animals running all around. The woman screamed! Were these rats?

By now, the woman's husband had arrived down in the basement. Laughing, he told her that these little animals were just possums.

And, likely, Mama Possum must have gotten spooked and made a hasty departure, leaving in her wake her babies scrambling across the basement floor. Animal control came and said the babies were too young to live on their own. The official said she rehabilitated animals and would take care of them.

It was several months later that possums once more appeared, this time in the garage. The possums were climbing the walls. The woman called animal control again. She was told the possums were old enough this time to live on their own and could be relocated. Animal control said, "Do not be afraid of them. They rarely have rabies, because to get rabies, they have to be in a fight with a rabid animal and live. And possums never live."

The woman was told by animal control how to catch the possums (by their tails), and she was provided a cage. Thus began the possum relocation project.

Each morning, the woman began to look for possums on the walls of the garage, on the floor of the garage, and even in the garbage can. Plucking up the possums, she put them in the car and then drove five miles down the park road for the relocation project. Searching for possums became part of the morning ritual. In fact, she and her husband became quite used to having the possums around.

But the woman knew that possums were not pets.

A solution had to be found. The woman and her husband figured out how Mama Possum was getting into the house, but they needed to catch her in the house to seal the entrance.

While the family was on vacation, the house sitter found Mama Possum with another litter in a hamper full of old towels in the basement. The woman told the house sitter to take the possums, hamper and all, deep into the woods of another county to relocate them.

So Mama Possum went to live in the woods twenty-five miles away. And Mama Possum was never coming back.

MORAL

A path into a house does not guarantee a home.

SASHA

Open my eyes, that I may see glimpses of truth thou has for me.
—From a hymn by Clara H. Scott

It was love at first sight. My son, William, had taken his first glimpse of a Siberian husky who was up for adoption.

He had been asking for another dog for some months, but the answer was always no. Eventually that changed to a maybe, if a dog could be found that was house-trained, spayed, loved cats, and didn't have heartworms.

The very next week, I saw a notice in the veterinarian's office for such a beast, told William's dad at lunch, and he said, "His prayers were answered. Pick up the dog."

So William got his new pet, Sasha.

From the moment our new husky jumped into our car, she did everything right. She climbed up on the seat with William and put her head on his lap, and it seemed like an ideal match between a boy and his dog.

On arriving home, all of us fell in love with this smart, beautiful husky. She was quiet and loving. She spent time with each member of the family, making all of us feel special. She made peace with the cats and the other dog. Sasha seemed very smart, recognizing her new name and coming when called.

Of most importance, she never had an accident in the house, unlike our other dog, Brutus, who had many accidents for fifteen years.

Sasha slept with William and followed the children around dutifully. She knew her place. We grew fonder and fonder of her each day.

In the second week that Sasha was in her new home, many things began to change. It all started in slow and subtle ways. At first, we found a box of tissues chewed up and strewn around the room. William laughed as he cleaned up the mess. He wasn't laughing by the time he cleaned up four more boxes of tissues in two days. Then, Sasha moved on to chew up our favorite doorstop duck, which had been in the family for ten years. She chewed toys, rugs, and our favorite beach blanket. I guess love is blind until one's favorite blanket is chewed up.

However, chewing was not her only bad habit. She didn't bark, but she howled to get what she wanted. It was a piercing, wolf like howl. It was cute at first, but then it became very irritating when the kids were doing their homework or when we were watching television. Sasha seemed to turn from a perfect dog to a pain overnight.

Another bad habit was Sasha's running. She charged up and down our steps, almost knocking us down. She dashed around the house and tried to escape out the front door.

Sasha also figured out a way out of the fence. She easily climbed over the five-foot fence. (I later found out that huskies need a six-foot fence.)

The times she succeeded in getting loose, we always panicked and kept yelling her name outside. Eventually, we put a dog bell on her, so we could hear her return. The bell would be faint and then get louder and louder until she appeared. Several times we got into the car looking for her, and on our return, she would be sitting on the front porch.

It slowly dawned on us that a husky's basic nature as a work dog caused this tendency to run. She was bred to pull sleds.

Because there were no sleds to pull, she had to use up her almost-limitless energy.

William was disillusioned by her destructive behavior. Actually, all of us were. What were we going to do with this new dog who was here to stay?

We decided to take some positive steps to cope with Sasha. We began walking her at least a mile a day to wear her out. We dealt with the howling by feeding her on a strict schedule. We disciplined her in the kindest ways we could. We watched her carefully to eliminate any signs of destructive behavior.

As we began treating Sasha in a more realistic way, all of us became more adjusted and happy. We learned to accept one another just the way we are.

MORAL

Love is blind, but it is also the tie that binds.

SASHA'S STROKE

Through sickness and health 'til death do us part.
— From traditional wedding vows.

I was at a medical conference when my husband called me in Washington, DC, to tell me that he thought Sasha had a stroke.

Being fifty miles away and having traveled by train, I rushed out of the conference, threw my clothes in the suitcase, and raced to the train station.

When I arrived home, Sasha was too weak to get up. Her legs were splayed on the floor. I was devastated. I called my son, William, who was already out of college, to come home immediately and meet us at the vet's office. I knew that the probability of Sasha having to be put to sleep was great.

When my helper, Marilyn Perry, came to help me, we put Sasha on a blanket and dragged her to the door. Then something miraculous happened. Sasha seemed to sense what was happening and shakily walked to the car. We lifted her in and raced to the vet's office.

I had already called ahead and told the vet what might have to happen. William got to the vet's office around the same time. Much to our amazement, Sasha shakily walked into the office. All of us were in tears.

The vet took one look at Sasha and said that she had indeed suffered a stroke, but to take her home. "It wasn't her time."

So Sasha returned home, and there she lived for six months. She was a very weak dog, but she managed to be able to walk outside. She did, however, for the first time in her life have accidents in the house.

We coped with all of her old-age problems as best as we could. After all of the years of joy and comfort that she had given us, she deserved no less.

And frankly, I treated her like a nursing home patient for a lot of the time. I didn't mind. Really, it was my honor. I owed it to this beautiful animal that enriched our family so.

And then it was time. She went to the *Rainbow Bridge*.

MORAL

Health is wealth, but old deserves gold!

KITTY, THE STRAY WHO STAYED

There's no place like home!
—John Howard Payne

Our last cat, Prissy, had just died about a month before. We had adopted homeless cats over a twenty-year period, and I felt we were done with cats.

Then both my husband and I had multiple sightings of a black cat walking through the yard.

I said to my husband, "Don't feed her; don't talk to her. Just ignore her." We didn't pay any attention to the cat for two weeks.

But then, being the animal lovers we are, one day I gave in and called her. "Here, kitty, kitty," I said, and she came right to me. It was delightful to see the cat purring all over my husband as she sat on his lap.

Could that cat instinctively detect that we would not harm her? That we had a long history of adopting animals?

But something bothered me. Maybe this cat was so friendly because she was someone else's pet. I was bound and determined to find the cat's owner. I put ads in the paper, with no results.

So, resigned that we would adopt yet another stray cat, I tried to get our dog, who loved to chase cats, familiar with the kitty before I brought her in the house. I put the dog on the back screened porch and the cat in the fenced yard. There was lots of barking, and then the barking stopped. I thought as I walked to the porch that my mission was accomplished. However, what I saw was the screen busted out of the porch, the dog in the backyard, and kitty on the front porch.

Soon afterward, the phone rang. It definitely was the cat's owner. In the description of the cat, I had left out an identifying characteristic the cat possessed, and this caller knew what it was—a small tuft of white hair on her chest.

I was both sad and joyful that we had found the owner. The owner came the next day to retrieve her cat. This kitty had been gone for three months. But what happened next was very surprising. The cat would not go with the owner. No matter how much this cat's owner talked to her, and at some point held her, this cat jumped down and ran away.

The owner felt crushed. I had to call again with my "here, kitty, kitty" routine, put her in my car, and the owner finally coaxed her into a cat carrier after talking to the cat for fifteen minutes in my car.

Feeling good about finding the owner didn't last long. The kitty was back after traveling a distance of some three miles, which included crossing two heavily trafficked major highways.

Now what?

The owner told me that she had gotten a new dog that this kitty didn't like, that all her dogs and cats could come and go out of the doggie door, but this kitty was *not* a house cat. And she didn't know what to tell us to do now.

The day that the kitty came back, workers were here putting on a new roof on the house for a week. That totally freaked the kitty out, and she would not come to me either. She stayed across the street. So not knowing what to do, I bought food for her for five months and took it to the neighbor's house.

All of this time, my husband missed her. Finally, another "here, kitty, kitty" got her up the driveway. And there she stayed, on our front porch.

We called her Kitty. It seemed the sensible thing to do. I don't think we really admitted that Kitty was our cat for the first four years. But our cat she was. We were just kidding ourselves.

Porch life was fine in the spring, summer, and fall, but the winters were harsh for an outdoor cat. I rigged up a comforter tent structure on the porch for Kitty. She didn't seem to mind. She seemed to appreciate her little corner of the world on that porch. She had a garage she could have gone in, but she much preferred the porch's wide-open view of the front yard.

Kitty brought a lot of comfort to my husband and to me because we also liked to sit on the porch.

She protected me from a fox one day, risking her own life. The baby fox was approaching me from the garage. I was able to scare the fox, but it doubled back and came up the front walk where Kitty was always looking. She stood her ground and scared away the fox. Kitty seemed so proud of herself, and I was so touched and grateful.

Kitty was a good watch-cat. When we would drive up the driveway, she would meet us at the garage, with the message in Kitty language, "All is well," which also brought us a lot of comfort.

Kitty lived on our porch for eight years. She had found herself a porch home, and we had to admit that we really liked having her around.

MORAL

There is no place like home, even if it is a porch.

THE DEVOTED CAT LOVER

Love is sustained by action, a pattern of devotion in the things we do for each other every day.
—Nicholas Sparks

 Gobble was a beautiful brown, short-haired tabby cat. This cat was rescued and adopted into a loving home. The name Gobble was given to her for the way she liked to gobble her food. Gobble enjoyed her new home, her new pet parents, and her basic nature as a cat. She loved her independence and loved the outdoors. She would spend hours walking, enjoying the sunshine, and exploring her new yard, and then cuddle with her pet parents at night. She was especially close to her pet mother.

As she grew older, Gobble became affected by a common medical condition occurring in older cats, kidney disease and failure. Sometimes a cat can be given more time with Vet ordered help of fluids under the skin.

Gobble's pet mother was going to try and extend Gobble's life. She started giving the cat fluids under her skin to help flush out the poisons building up in her system. This procedure had to be done every other day. And it would not have been successful without two very important considerations.

First, the commitment of the pet parent is of prime importance. This commitment entails time, expense, and an attitude of humble service to a cat. Gobble's pet parent had continued to go to extraordinary means to help her.

Second, this treatment also demanded the cooperation of the cat involved. Now, if anyone knows cats, how many cats would trust their owner enough for them to put a needle under their skin every other day? And how many cats could sit still for four minutes while a bag of IV fluids would run into the cat? But Gobble and her pet mother were devoted to each other.

Gobble's pet mother gave her these treatments for six years. Gobble enjoyed a good quality of life all of this time, sitting in the sun, taking walks, and sitting in her yard. Gobble and her pet mother enjoyed their time together. Her pet parent talked to her and stroked her, and Gobble purred, as they both seemed to say to each other, "I love you."

MORAL

Devotion is as devotion does.

PEPPER

I once was lost, but now I'm found…
—From the hymn "Amazing Grace"

Pepper and her siblings were tossed on the side of the road, but they were rescued by an animal organization. She was given a foster home, and Pepper was the sickest and weakest of all the brothers and sisters. But with love and attention, Pepper made an amazing recovery, and she was ready for her forever home.

At the same time, a woman had to cope with a breast cancer diagnosis and two surgeries, and she started a holistic wellness lifestyle. She walked three miles a day and needed a walking buddy.

As grace works in our lives, Pepper was put up for adoption at Petsmart the very day the woman went in to buy pet food. It was love at first sight for the woman and this dog. After talking it over with her husband, Pepper was adopted.

Pepper ran away the first day she was adopted. The animal rescue people came from thirty-five miles away and had to call Pepper to lure her back. They asked the woman a critical question, "Do you still want to keep her?" She answered, "Yes."

All was well for six months until the woman took Pepper to Randolph Macon College (RMC) for parents' weekend. She did not want to leave her at home, because Pepper had a destructive side.

Pepper saw a squirrel, got out of her harness, and ran off. The woman was devastated. She put fliers up all over the college, walked miles that weekend calling her name, and had to go home without her.

That week in between her teaching at the community college, the woman went back to RMC and took her husky, Sasha, with her for the scent, and kept looking for Pepper. She stayed in a fraternity SAE on campus by day (those fraternity boys were very kind to the woman) and close to the campus at night.

The woman hunted all over that city, walking miles each day. She went out and did the same in the middle of the night. She had Pepper's favorite sock and also dog bones all over the college. No Pepper was found, but there were sightings.

It was fall break, and again the woman had to go home without Pepper. The next day, Saturday, the woman got a call that the dog shelter found her. She and her husband drove to the shelter, but sadly, it was a Pepper look-alike.

The next day, Sunday, the woman got a call that Pepper was sighted crossing a major road. The woman hopped in the car and sped to the college. Because it was a Sunday, instead of calling for the dog, she sang hymns. One of them was "Amazing Grace," including the words, "I once was lost, but now I'm found, was blind, but now I see."

Way behind the dormitory was a lot of debris, and the woman was singing the fourth verse of "Amazing Grace": "Through many trials, storms, and snares, I have already come. But grace has led me safe thus far, and grace will lead me home." To her amazement, Pepper came to her. The woman put food on the ground, and when Pepper went to eat it, the woman tackled her to get the collar on her neck.

Pepper, the woman, and the husky came out of the woods into the sun with great joy and thankfulness.

MORAL

If God's grace gives you a home, run to it, not from it.

A GIRL AND HER DOG

If God is for us, who can be against us?
—Romans 8:3

Once upon a time there lived a very unhappy thirteen-year-old girl. She was constantly picked on and made fun of by the other kids at school. It now has a name—bullying. What made the bullying even worse in the girl's mind was that it started at Sunday school, and from there it extended to the junior high school.

They laughed at her because she had glasses, pimples on her face, braces, and sometimes wore not-so-stylish clothes. Most of all, they laughed because she had just changed schools and she was considered an outsider.

The only comfort the girl had through this trying time in her life was praying to God and getting comfort through being with her dog, Checkers.

Checkers was really her brother's dog; however, the girl and her dog, were inseparable.

Checkers would sleep in the girl's room, lie next to her in the house, and take long walks with the girl after school. They would walk to an old cemetery, and the girl would sit down with Checkers, telling the dog about her horrible days, sometimes even crying to this dog. Checkers was her only friend.

For the girl, things got worse at school. On one particularly bad day, the bullying intensified. The girl found a squished egg salad sandwich in her Latin book. Then she had a chair scooted out from under her in the cafeteria. And then other kids called her a horrible name—"Hatchet Face"—and avoided her in the halls like she had some disease.

After the girl came home from school that day, she went straight to Checkers. The dog sensed the urgency in the girl's voice and the sadness in her face. Checkers briskly walked with the girl to their favorite spot, and Checkers laid her head down on the girl's lap as she talked to God. The girl asked God why this was happening to her. Would this ever pass? Didn't she have something special under that ugly face and plain clothes? Why weren't people looking past the outside and looking on the inside of this kind, loving girl? Isn't that what really counts?

In a still, small voice God gave her the answers. She realized that she had to hang in there and this terrible time in her life would soon pass. Maybe she could try a little harder, making friends with the right people at school. Maybe she could try to help someone else in need, and this would help her forget about her own problems. Whatever she tried, she knew that she wasn't alone in her ordeal.

Checkers, who was sitting patiently, leaned over and licked the girl's face and nuzzled her arm.

Checkers confirmed what God was trying to say.

MORAL

Spell it forward or backward; God is still man's best friend.

HERE IS THE REST OF
THE STORY IN SYNOPSIS
OF THESE BEASTS.

Brutus lived until he was seventeen years old. The dining room rug was replaced.

Dude and Rebel were the dogs of Philip Briel Lloyd, my stepson. They were both adopted from Fredericksburg's dog mart. We still have many rocks in the front yard Dude fetched.

Here is a picture of all four dogs around 1974 getting their Thanksgiving dinner

Lady lived to be about twelve years old. Right before our son William was born, Stacy bred Pretty Lady, and her pups Hana and Tul (one and two in Korean) were born when William was six weeks old. Viewing that whole experience of an Ob-Gyn watching and worrying about that birth of those pups after he had delivered around six thousand babies at that point was hysterically funny.

Lady and I entered and won several dog mart contests. She dressed up as the spirit of seventy-six with Brutus and me, and we won that contest, too. She was also dressed up as a bride, a hula dancer, and an Indian at other dog marts.

Gidget was a dog that needed a home. She was five years old and already obese.

Ricky was the dog of my aunt, Lillian Wilson, and my cousin, Carol Wilson. He died thinking he was a person.

The cats involved in the mice story eagerly awaited the next mouse in the house.

Whitepaws slept with William most of the time. (This is soon after he learned how to love.)

Whitepaws lived until he was fifteen years old. Our oldest rescued cat, he had a revered place in our animal house. It was always an honor when he sat next to one of us. The day before he died, when William was  home from college, with little strength left, he jumped on the bed and slept with his beloved friend, William, one more time.

The ducks were the pets of my husband as a small boy in Richmond, Virginia, in 1935.

Pete was the parakeet of my Aunt Lillian Wilson.

The gerbil story involves those I owned when I first moved to Fredericksburg, Virginia, from Cleveland in 1969.

Casey was the hamster of Susan Hodgdon of Fredericksburg and Kentucky.

Sasha lived until she was fifteen years old. She was adored by the whole family as long as she lived. None of us can walk down the street and see a husky and not think of Sasha, and we all get a smile on our face. She was instrumental in finding her lost pet mate, Pepper, walking miles and miles in her old age. She was the most beautiful dog who loved the snow and would stay out for hours making igloos in the backyard.

Pepper was my walking buddy until arthritis made me give up walking for exercise. She then enjoyed the backyard for the rest of her life. Pepper was our last dog.

Kitty was our last cat.

Gobble was a pet of my friend Suzanne McIntosh, who cared for her until she went to the *Rainbow Bridge* at age seventeen.

This is a picture of Checkers with my brother, Jonathan William Holasek, and with my dad, William Holasek who spent a lot of time caring for her.

I never forgot the bullying I received as a child in Parma, Ohio. And I want people to know that it leaves scars for life. I told my children, and now I am telling my grandchildren to never engage in any kind of bullying. They can now read my story for themselves.

I take great comfort in the poem "The Rainbow Bridge." Here is a link to this beautiful poem: https://rainbowsbridge.com/poem.htm.

All of these beasts have enriched my life and the lives of my family members beyond measure. My whole family carries on the legacy of adopting pets.

ABOUT THE AUTHOR

Marilyn Holasek Lloyd is an RN who has experienced many different careers. She was a psychiatric nurse, an Ob-Gyn office nurse, and a patient advocate. Upon receiving her Bachelors of Liberal Studies degree from Mary Washington College (MWC), she became a holistic health public speaker and an adjunct instructor.

After her Masters of Liberal Studies degree at MWC, (now The University of Mary Washington), she worked as an adjunct instructor in the English Department at Germanna Community College, teaching college composition, *Children's Literature* and *Film and Literature.*

All of her careers ignited a passion for writing and she wrote book reviews and essays for *The Free Lance Star* in Fredericksburg, Virginia, for several years. After her breast cancer diagnosis, she wrote a blog for dadamo.com and a column for Nicholas Regush's website, *Redflagsdaily* (not in print).

Marilyn's blogs are *Coping and Commentary* and *Breast Cancer Journeys on Wordpress.* She can also be found on *Google* and *Facebook.*